I0413267

NRC headquarters offices are located in Rockville, Maryland.

Contents

Radioactive Waste: An Introduction 1

High-Level Radioactive Waste 7

What is high-level waste? 7

What is the role of NRC? 7

How hazardous is high-level waste? 7

How and where is the waste stored? 9

How much high-level waste is there? 13

How and where will high-level waste be disposed of? 14

(continued)

Contents

Low-Level Radioactive Waste 19

    What is low-level waste? 19

    Where does low-level waste come from? 20

    What is the role of NRC? 24

    How hazardous is low-level waste? 24

    How is low-level waste stored? 25

    How and where is low-level waste disposed of? 26

Mill Tailings 31

Additional Information 34

Radioactive Waste: An Introduction

Radioactive wastes are the leftovers from the use of nuclear materials for the production of electricity, diagnosis and treatment of disease, and other purposes.

The materials are either naturally occurring or man-made. Certain kinds of radioactive materials, and the wastes produced from using these materials, are subject to regulatory control by the federal government or the states.

The Department of Energy (DOE) is responsible for radioactive waste related to nuclear weapons production and certain research activities. The Nuclear Regulatory Commission (NRC) and some states regulate commercial radioactive waste that results from the production of electricity and other non-military uses of nuclear material.

Various other federal agencies, such as the Environmental Protection Agency, the Department of Transportation, and the Department of Health and Human Services, also have a role in the regulation of radioactive material.

The NRC regulates the management, storage and disposal of radioactive waste produced as a result of NRC-licensed activities. The agency has entered into agreements with 32 states, called Agreement States, to allow these states to regulate the management, storage and disposal of certain nuclear waste.

Nuclear power plants, such as this Calvert Cliffs plant near Lusby, Maryland, produce electricity and, as a byproduct, produce radioactive waste.

The commercial radioactive waste that is regulated by the NRC or the Agreement States and that is the subject of this brochure is of three basic types: high-level waste, mill tailings, and low-level waste.

High-level radioactive waste consists of "irradiated" or used nuclear reactor fuel (i.e., fuel that has been used in a reactor to produce electricity). The used reactor fuel is in a solid form consisting of small fuel pellets in long metal tubes.

Mill tailings wastes are the residues remaining after the processing of natural ore to extract uranium and thorium.

Commercial radioactive wastes that are not high-level wastes or uranium and thorium milling wastes are classified as low-level radioactive waste. The low-level wastes can include radioactively contaminated protective clothing, tools, filters, rags, medical tubes, and many other items.

NRC licensees are encouraged to manage their activities so as to limit the amount of radioactive waste they produce. Techniques include avoiding the spread of radioactive contamination, surveying items to ensure that they are radioactive before placing them in a radioactive waste container, using care to avoid mixing contaminated waste with other trash, using radioactive materials whose radioactivity diminishes quickly and limiting radioactive material usage to the minimum necessary to establish the objective.

Licensees take steps to reduce the volume of radioactive waste after it has been produced. Common means are compaction and incineration. Approximately 59 NRC licensees are authorized to incinerate certain low-level wastes, although most incineration is performed by a small number of commercial incinerators.

The radioactivity of nuclear waste decreases with the passage of time, through a process called radioactive decay. ("Radioactivity" refers to the spontaneous disintegration of an unstable atomic nucleus, usually accompanied by the emission of ionizing radiation.) The amount of time necessary to decrease the radioactivity of radioactive material to one-half the original amount is called the radioactive half-life of the radioactive material. Radioactive waste with a short half-life is often stored temporarily before disposal in order to reduce potential radiation doses to workers who handle and transport the waste, as well as to reduce the radiation levels at disposal sites.

In addition, NRC authorizes some licensees to store short-half-lived material until the radioactivity is indistinguishable from ambient radiation levels, and then dispose of the material as non-radioactive waste.

Currently, there are no permanent disposal facilities in the United States for high-level nuclear waste; therefore commercial high-level waste (spent fuel) is in temporary storage, mainly at nuclear power plants.

Most uranium mill tailings are disposed of in place or near the mill, after constructing a barrier of a material such as clay on top of the pile to prevent radon from escaping into the atmosphere and covering the mill tailings pile with soil, rocks or other materials to prevent erosion.

For low-level waste, three commercial land disposal facilities are available, but they accept waste only from certain states or accept only limited types of low-level wastes. The remainder of the low-level waste is stored primarily at the site where

This low-level radioactive waste disposal site in Richland, Washington, accepts wastes from the Northwest and Rocky Mountain states.

it was produced, such as at hospitals, research facilities, clinics and nuclear power plants.

The following sections of this pamphlet provide separate discussions on high-level and low-level radioactive waste and mill tailings.

Radioactive Waste: Production, Storage, Disposal

High-Level Radioactive Waste

What is high-level waste?

After uranium fuel has been used in a reactor for a while, it is no longer as efficient in splitting its atoms and producing heat to make electricity. It is then called "spent" nuclear fuel. About one-fourth to one-third of the total fuel load is spent and is removed from the reactor every 12 to 18 months and replaced with fresh fuel. The spent nuclear fuel is high-level radioactive waste.

What is the role of NRC?

The NRC regulates all commercial reactors in the United States, including nuclear power plants that produce electricity, and university research reactors. The agency regulates the possession, transportation, storage and disposal of spent fuel produced by the nuclear reactors.

How hazardous is high-level waste?

Spent nuclear fuel is highly radioactive and potentially very harmful. Standing near unshielded spent fuel could be fatal due to the high radiation levels. Ten years after removal of spent fuel from a reactor, the radiation dose 1 meter away from a typical spent fuel assembly exceeds 20,000 rems per hour. A dose of 5,000 rems would be expected to cause immediate incapacitation and death within one week.

Some of the radioactive elements in spent fuel have short half-lives (for example, iodine-131 has an 8-day half-life) and therefore their radioactivity decreases rapidly. However, many of the radioactive elements in spent fuel have long half-lives. For example, plutonium-239 has a half-life of 24,000 years, and plutonium-240 has a half-life of 6,800 years. Because it contains these long half-lived radioactive elements, spent fuel must be isolated and controlled for thousands of years.

A second hazard of spent fuel, in addition to high radiation levels, is the extremely remote possibility of an accidental "criticality," or self-sustained fissioning and splitting of the atoms of uranium and plutonium.

NRC regulations therefore require stringent design, testing and monitoring in the handling and storage of spent fuel to ensure that the risk of this type of accident is extremely unlikely. For example, special control materials (usually boron) are placed in spent fuel containers to prevent a criticality from occurring. Nuclear engineers and physicists carefully analyze and monitor the conditions of handling and storage of spent fuel to guard further against an accident.

A barrier or radiation protection shield must always be placed between spent nuclear fuel and human beings.

Water, concrete, lead, steel, depleted uranium or other suitable materials calculated to be sufficiently protective by trained engineers and health physicists, and verified by radiation measurements, are typically used as radiation shielding for spent nuclear fuel.

Most spent fuel from nuclear power plants is stored under water, as shown at the Diablo Canyon plant in California.

How and where is the waste stored?

Spent fuel may be stored in either a wet or dry environment. In addition, it may be stored either at the reactor where it was used or away from the reactor at another site.

The various techniques are as follows:

Wet Storage

Currently most spent nuclear fuel is safely stored in specially designed pools at individual reactor sites around the country. The water-pool option involves storing spent fuel in rods under at least 20 feet of water, which provides adequate

9

shielding from the radiation for anyone near the pool. The rods are moved into the water pools from the reactor along the bottom of water canals, so that the spent fuel always is shielded to protect workers.

A typical spent fuel rod is about 12 feet long and 3/4 inch in diameter. The rods are arranged in somewhat square arrays, known as fuel assemblies, that range in size from an array of 6 rods by 6 rods to an array of 17 rods by 17 rods. The fuel pools vary in size from a capacity of 216 to 8,083 fuel assemblies.

Most pools were originally designed to store several years worth of spent fuel. Due to delays in developing disposal facilities for the spent fuel, licensees have redesigned and rebuilt equipment in the pools over the years to allow a greater number of spent fuel rods to be stored. However, this storage option is limited by the size of the spent fuel pool and the need to keep individual fuel rods from getting too close to other rods and initiating a criticality or nuclear reaction.

Dry Storage

If pool capacity is reached, licensees may move toward use of above-ground dry storage casks. The first dry storage installation was licensed by the NRC in 1986. In this method, spent fuel is surrounded by inert gas inside a container called a cask. The casks can be made of metal or concrete, and some can be used for both storage and transportation. They are either placed horizontally or stand vertically on a concrete pad.

Seventeen nuclear power plants are currently storing spent fuel under the dry storage option.

Spent fuel may be stored in dry casks either horizontally, as shown at the H.B. Robinson nuclear power plant in South Carolina, or vertically, as shown at the Surry nuclear power plant in Virginia.

Away-from-Reactor Storage

General Electric Company has a facility to store spent fuel away from reactors, using the wet storage pool technology, at Morris, Illinois. GE received a license to receive and store nuclear material at this facility in 1971. The facility is essentially full, and the company has completed contracts with specific utilities (under which it had agreed to accept their used fuel) and has no plans to accept additional spent fuel.

Storage Differences

Both pool storage and dry storage are safe methods, but there are significant differences. Pool storage requires a greater and more consistent operational vigilance on the part of utilities or other licensees and the satisfactory performance of many mechanical systems using pumps, piping and instrumentation.

Dry storage, which is almost completely passive, is simpler, uses fewer support systems and offers fewer opportunities for things to go wrong through human or mechanical error. Dry storage is not suitable for fuel until the fuel has been out of the reactor for a few years and the amount of heat generated by radioactive decay has been reduced.

Monitored Retrievable Storage

The Nuclear Waste Policy Act (NWPA) of 1982 authorized the Department of Energy (DOE) to construct a monitored retrievable storage (MRS) facility for storage of high-level waste, with certain restrictions.

Representatives of state and local governments and Indian tribes and members of the public would be invited to participate in meetings on an MRS facility.

NRC would publish notice of receipt of DOE's application to build an MRS facility and hold a public hearing, if requested, before issuance of the license.

How much high-level waste is there?

About 160,000 spent fuel assemblies, containing 45,000 tons of spent fuel from nuclear power plants, are currently in storage in the United States. Of these, about 156,500 assemblies are stored at nuclear power plants, and approximately 3,500 assemblies are stored at away-from-reactor storage facilities, such as the General Electric plant at Morris, Illinois. The vast majority of the assemblies are stored in water pools, and less than 5% are stored in dry casks.

About 7,800 used fuel assemblies are taken out of reactors each year and are stored until a disposal facility becomes available.

If all the 160,000 spent fuel assemblies currently in storage were assembled in one place, they would only cover a football field about 5 1/2 yards high.

How and where will the high-level waste be disposed of?

DOE is developing plans for a permanent disposal facility for spent fuel from nuclear power plants (as well as for the high-level waste that has been produced by the nation's nuclear weapons production activities).

Congress has directed DOE to focus on a proposed site at Yucca Mountain, Nevada, for the disposal facility. This has aroused some controversy, particularly with state and local authorities.

Studies are still underway to determine if the site is adequate for permanent disposal of the high-level waste. NRC has a rigorous regulatory program for review of these ongoing DOE site investigations.

DOE would design, build and operate the facility, subject to federal regulations and oversight by the NRC. The NRC must approve the site and design for the disposal facility, as well as inspect it during construction and operation.

The Nuclear Waste Policy Act directed the Department of Energy to study Yucca Mountain, Nevada, to determine whether it would be suitable for disposal of high-level radioactive waste.

Once DOE submits an application to construct a repository, the NWPA calls for NRC to complete its review within three years.

If the NRC authorizes construction, DOE will proceed with constructing the repository and would submit a license application update (containing additional details on design and construction of the facility) to the NRC. This would be followed by an NRC decision on whether to license operation of the repository.

NRC Safety Requirements

As required by the NWPA, the NRC has issued technical requirements and criteria for approving or disapproving DOE's application. These are contained in Part 60 of the NRC's regulations. Examples include:

■ Radiation doses during repository operations must be kept below regulatory limits. These limits are 100 millirems per year for members of the general public (which is about a third of the average American's annual dose from nature) and 5,000 millirems per year for workers.

■ Waste must be retrievable for 50 years after waste emplacement begins.

■ The container in which the high-level waste will be placed must maintain its integrity for 300 to 1,000 years.

■ The waste packages must not contain explosive or flammable materials or liquids that could endanger the repository.

Public Involvement

Representatives of state and local governments and Indian tribes are invited to participate in meetings on the high-level waste repository. Members of the public may attend as observers.

NRC will publish notice of receipt of DOE's application to build a repository and hold a public hearing before issuance of the construction authorization. When DOE submits an application to receive and possess high-level waste at the

LM-300 drill rig at Yucca Mountain, Nevada, obtained underground rock and soil samples that scientists examined to help determine site suitability for high-level waste disposal.

Tunnel boring machine excavated Yucca Mountain to allow analysis of underground conditions and suitability of site for high-level waste disposal.

facility, NRC will again announce receipt of the application and will publish notice of the opportunity for an optional additional public hearing.

The NRC has established an Internet web site to inform interested parties of upcoming meetings, including those on radioactive waste. The address is http://www.nrc.gov/public-involve/public-meetings.html on the Internet. Members of the public who do not have access to the Internet may obtain information on public meetings by calling 800-397-4209.

Low-Level Radioactive Waste

What is low-level waste?

Low-level radioactive waste includes items that have become contaminated with radioactive material or have become radioactive through exposure to neutron radiation. This waste is typically contaminated protective shoe covers and clothing, wiping rags, mops, filters, reactor water treatment residues, equipment and tools, luminous dials, medical tubes, swabs, injection needles, syringes, and laboratory animal carcasses and tissues. The most intensely radioactive wastes are typically found in the water treatment residues, discarded parts from nuclear reactors and small gauges containing radioactive material.

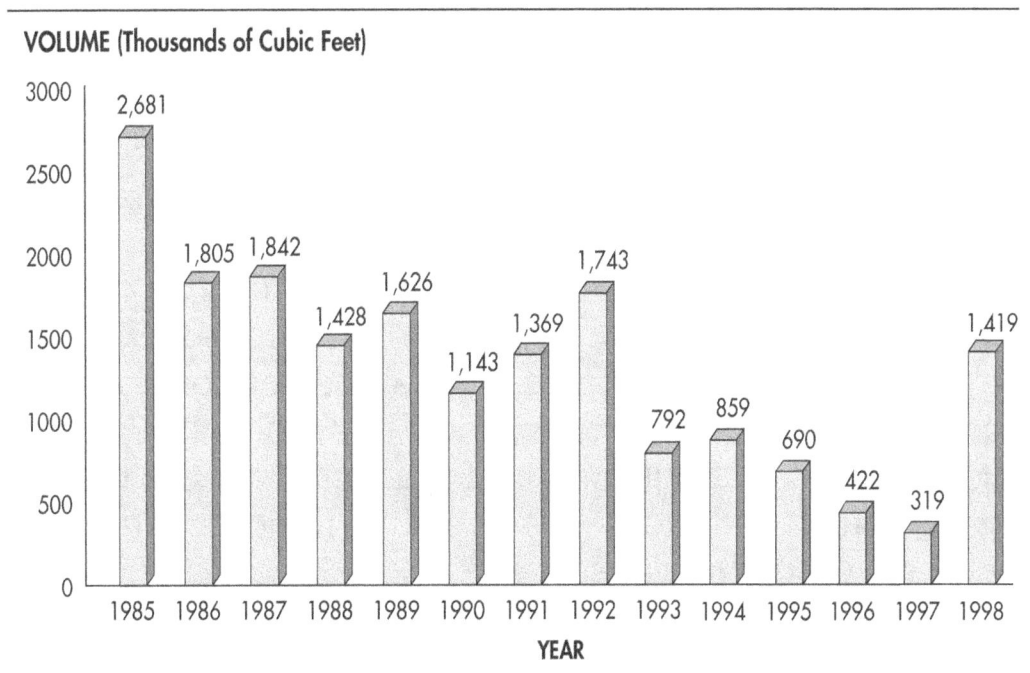

VOLUME (Thousands of Cubic Feet)

This chart shows the volume of low-level waste received at U.S. disposal facilities from 1985 to 1998.

The NRC has adopted a waste classification system for low-level radioactive waste based on its potential hazards, and has specified disposal and waste form requirements for each of the general classes of waste: Class A, Class B and Class C waste. Although the classification of waste can be complex, Class A waste generally contains lower concentrations of long half-lived radioactive material than Class B and C wastes.

Where does low-level waste come from?

In 1998, low-level waste disposal facilities received about 1,419 thousand cubic feet of commercially generated radioactive waste. Of this 14.8% came from nuclear reactors, 6.7% from industrial users, 2% from government sources (other than nuclear weapons sites), 0.3% from academic users, 0.1% from medical facilities, and the rest was undefined.

Nuclear Reactors

During normal operation of a nuclear reactor, some small amounts of radioactive material may be released into, or produced in, the water surrounding the fuel. Although reactor operators clean the water by using filters and resins, some of this material contaminates internal reactor components, such as pipes, pumps, valves, and filters, and other objects such as tools and equipment. Radiation from the reactor also produces radioactive waste that is removed when the reactor is decommissioned.

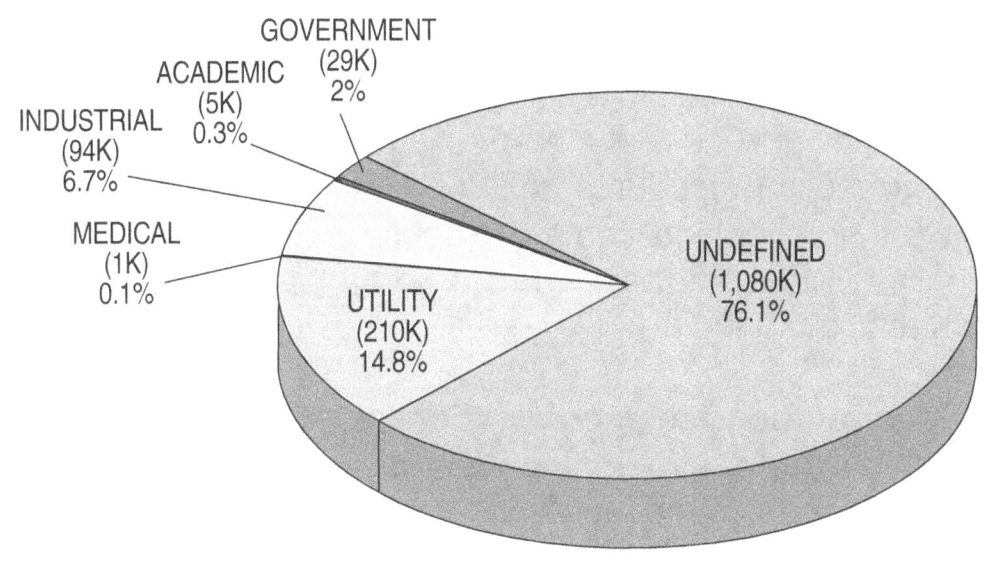

GOVERNMENT
(29K)
2%

ACADEMIC
(5K)
0.3%

INDUSTRIAL
(94K)
6.7%

MEDICAL
(1K)
0.1%

UTILITY
(210K)
14.8%

UNDEFINED
(1,080K)
76.1%

Total Amount Received –
1,419 thousand cubic feet

This chart shows the amount of low-level radioactive waste (in cubic feet) received from various sources in 1998 at U.S. disposal facilities.

To protect themselves, workers in contaminated areas at the power plants must sometimes wear protective gloves, clothing and, occasionally, respiratory equipment, which in turn could become contaminated.

These items become low-level waste, unless they are decontaminated. The filters and resins used to separate radioactive materials from water are also low-level waste. When the contaminated objects are no longer in use, they are placed in a specially marked low-level waste container for storage or disposal.

Medical Facilities

At medical facilities, radioactive materials are used in numerous diagnostic and therapeutic procedures for patients. During these procedures, test tubes, syringes, bottles, tubing and other objects come into contact with radioactive material. Some of the material remains in the objects, contaminating them.

In medical research, laboratory animals are sometimes injected with radioactive material for research purposes to combat diseases, such as AIDS and cancer. The animal carcasses containing the radioactive material become low-level radioactive waste and must be handled appropriately.

Hospitals may store waste containing radioactive material with short half lives until it decays to background radiation levels for ultimate disposal with non-radioactive medical waste. Waste containing longer-lived radioactive material is stored or sent to a low-level radioactive waste disposal facility.

Industry and Research Institutes

Commercial and industrial firms use radioactive materials to measure the thickness, density or volume of materials; to determine the age of prehistoric and geological objects; to examine welds and structures for flaws; to analyze wells for oil and gas exploration; and for various other types of research and development.

During research and chemical analysis, test tubes, bottles, tubing and process equipment come into contact with the

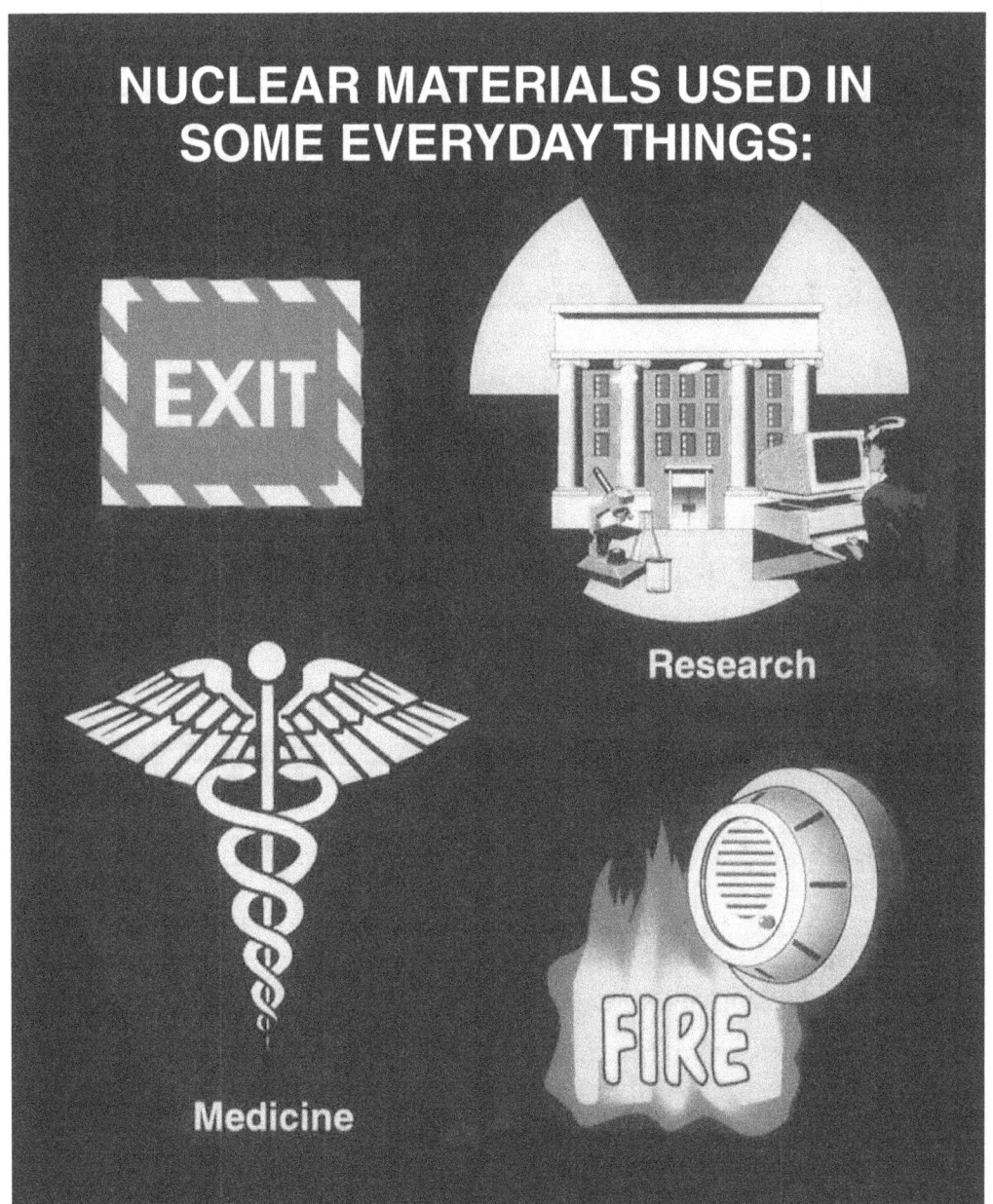

NUCLEAR MATERIALS USED IN SOME EVERYDAY THINGS:

Research

Medicine

FIRE

Use of nuclear materials for a variety of purposes, such as in exit signs, research, smoke detectors, and medicine, results in the production of nuclear waste.

radioactive material, become contaminated and are classified as low-level waste. Waste may also be produced during the manufacture of devices, such as certain gauges, luminous watches, exit signs and smoke detectors, that contain radioactive material.

What is the role of NRC?

The NRC regulates about 4,900 licenses for the possession and use of radioactive materials. In addition, 32 Agreement States regulate approximately 16,250 radioactive materials licenses. Agreement States are those states that have accepted responsibility, through agreement with the NRC, over the licensing of radioactive materials within their state.

The NRC and the Agreement States oversee licensees' management and disposal of radioactive waste products.

How hazardous is low-level waste?

The danger of exposure to radiation in low-level radioactive waste varies widely according to the types and concentration of radioactive material contained in the waste. Low-level waste containing some radioactive materials used in medical research, for example, is not particularly hazardous unless inhaled or consumed, and a person can stand near it without shielding. Low-level waste from processing water at a reactor, on the other hand, may be quite hazardous. For example, low-level waste could cause exposures that could lead to death or an increased risk of cancer.

How is low-level waste stored?

Storage of low-level radioactive waste requires an NRC or Agreement State license. NRC or Agreement State regulations require the waste to be stored in a manner that keeps radiation doses to workers and members of the public below NRC-specified levels. Licensees must further reduce these doses to levels that are as low as reasonably achievable. Actual doses, in most cases, are a small fraction of the NRC limits.

Low-level radioactive waste is packaged in containers appropriate to its level of hazard. Some low-level radioactive wastes require shielding with lead, concrete or other materials to protect workers and members of the public.

Workers are trained to maintain a safe distance from the more highly radioactive materials, to limit the amount of time they spend near the materials, and to monitor the waste to detect any releases.

Nuclear power plants may store waste in special buildings that provide an extra degree of shielding. Safe distances must be maintained between the buildings containing radioactive material and the fence restricting public access to licensee property.

Hospitals typically keep their waste stored in special containers or separate rooms.

Radioactive waste storage areas are posted to identify the radioactive waste so that workers and the public will not inadvertently enter the area.

Low-level waste may be stored to allow short-lived radio-nuclides to decay to innocuous levels and to provide safe-keeping when access to disposal sites is not available. The NRC believes storage can be safe over the short term as an interim measure, but favors disposal rather than storage over the long term.

How and where is low-level waste disposed of?

There are two low-level disposal facilities that accept a broad range of low-level wastes. They are located in Barnwell, South Carolina, and Richland, Washington.

This low-level waste disposal facility in Barnwell, South Carolina, buries waste underground.

In addition, Envirocare of Utah is licensed by the NRC to operate a facility near Clive, Utah, for disposal of uranium and thorium mill tailings. The facility also accepts certain other radioactive wastes under a State of Utah license. It primarily accepts low-level waste with small concentrations of radioactive material that are generated after a facility shuts down permanently and needs to remove a large bulk of contaminated material—such as contaminated soil or debris from demolished buildings—in preparation for license termination.

Four former low-level radioactive waste disposal sites are closed and no longer accept wastes. They are located in or near Sheffield, Illinois; Morehead, Kentucky; Beatty, Nevada; and West Valley, New York.

The low-level wastes at the Barnwell and Richland facilities and the four closed sites are or will be buried under several feet of soil in near-surface shallow trenches, usually in the containers in which they were shipped.

Laws and Regulations

The Low-Level Radioactive Waste Policy Amendments Act of 1985 made the states responsible for low-level radioactive waste disposal. It encouraged the states to enter into compacts that would allow several states to dispose of waste at a joint disposal facility. Most states have entered into compacts. However, to date no new disposal facilities have been built.

NRC and state regulations establish requirements for the siting, design and operation of disposal facilities, including buffer

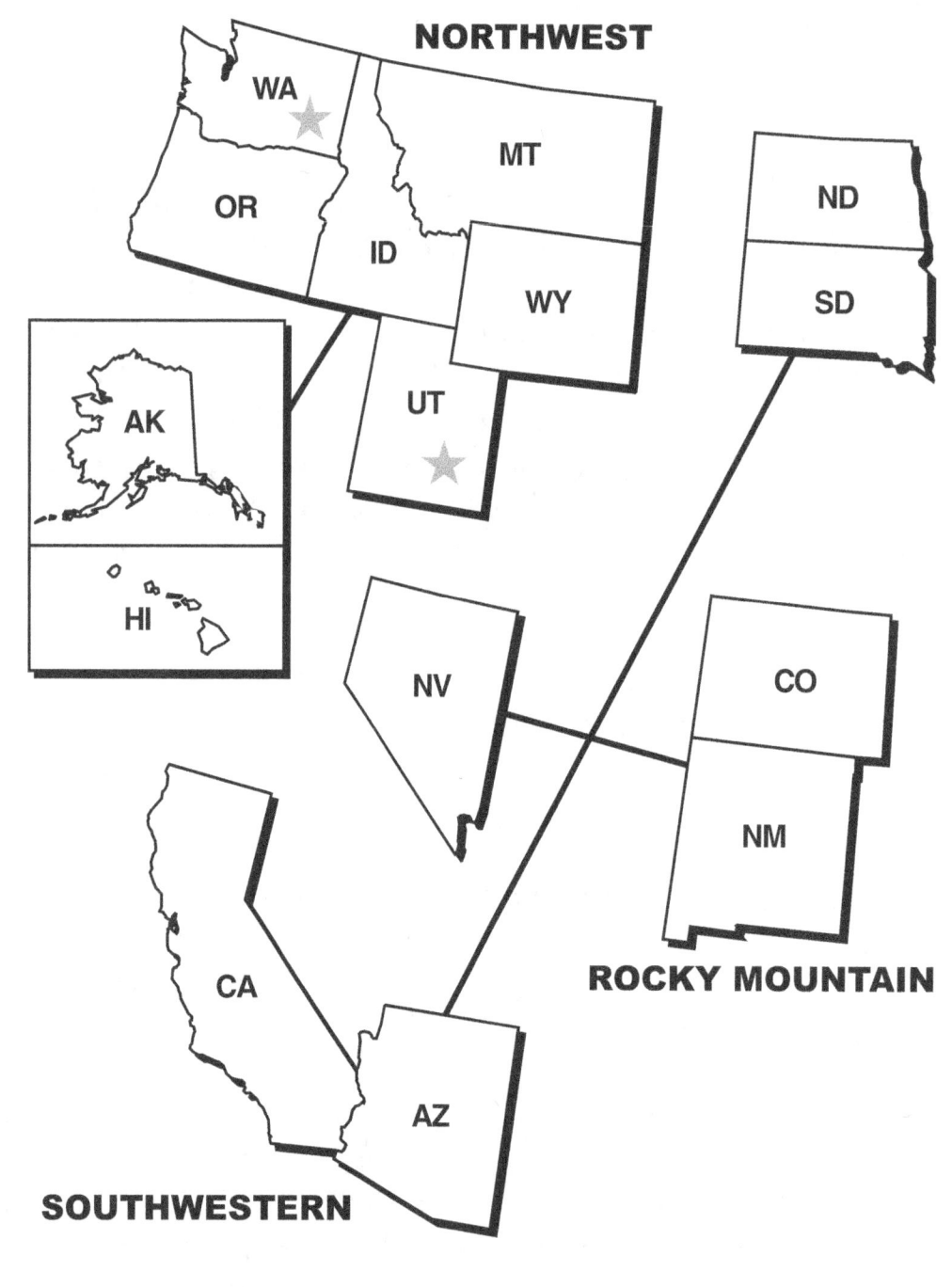

NORTHWEST

ROCKY MOUNTAIN

SOUTHWESTERN

Unaffiliated States

★ Operating LLW Disposal Sites

Note: National LLW volume for
1998 = 1,419 thousand cubic feet disposed

*Various states have banded together in low-level waste com-
pacts, with a plan to have one disposal facility per compact in*

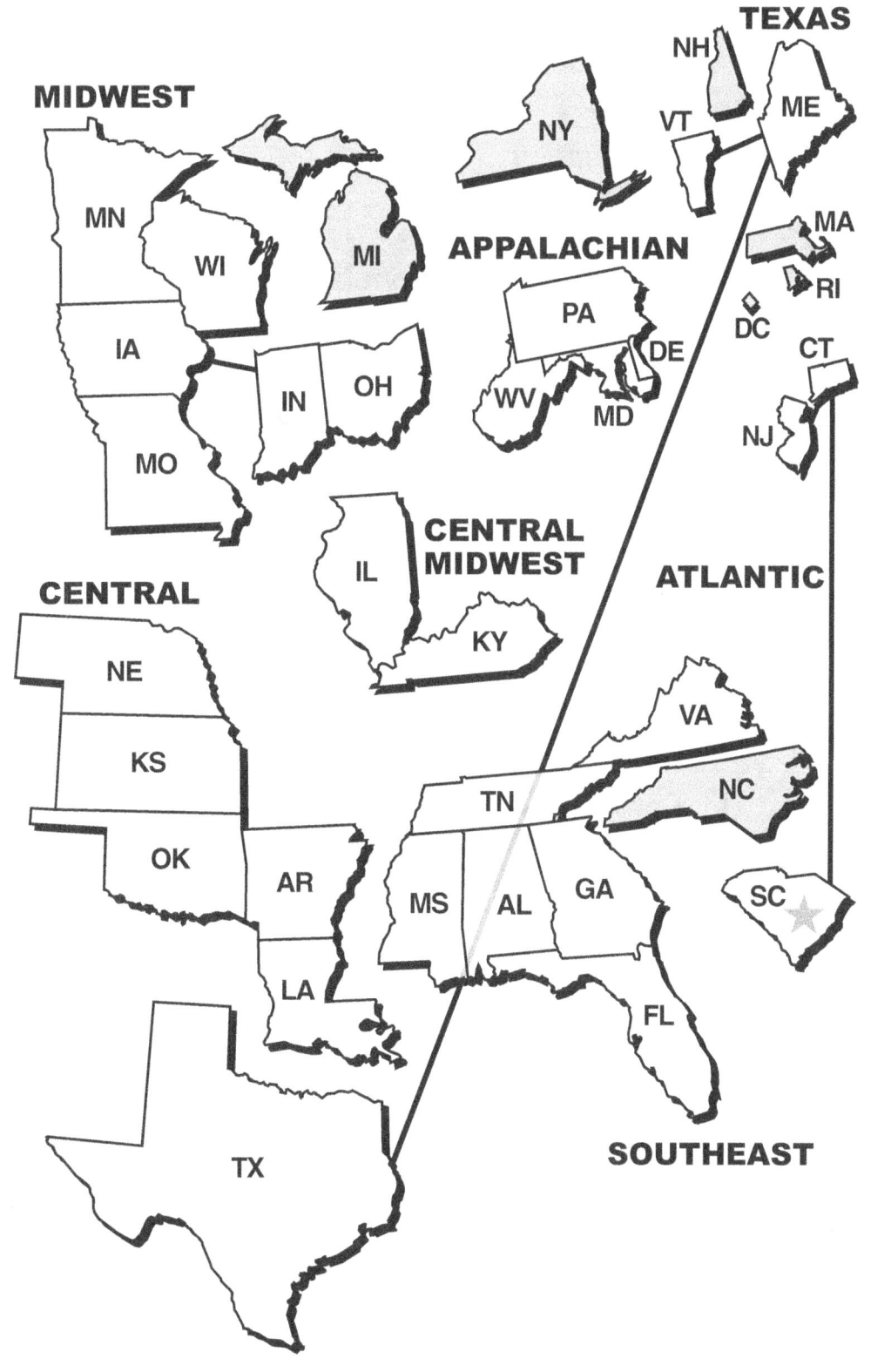

a selected host state. Currently the operational disposal sites are located in South Carolina, Utah and Washington.

zones of land surrounding and under the waste to permit monitoring and possible corrective actions.

When a disposal facility ceases operations, a post-closure period of maintenance and monitoring is required to confirm that the closed site is safely performing as expected before transfer to a government custodial agency for long-term control. Access to the site may be restricted for a long time, but NRC and state regulations do not allow reliance on institutional controls after 100 years following site closure. After 100 years, passive controls, such as custodial care, waste markers and land records, will be relied on to prevent disturbance of the emplaced waste.

Public Involvement

NRC and state procedures for development of a new low-level waste disposal facility provide several opportunities for public involvement, including:

■ Public review and comment on a license application;
■ Participation in the license review by the state or tribal governing body;
■ Public review and comment on the required draft environmental impact statement;
■ An opportunity for public hearings on the initial license and subsequent amendments;
■ Attendance at any of the NRC's meetings with the license applicant.

Mill Tailings

Tailing wastes are generated during the milling of certain ores to extract uranium and thorium. These wastes have relatively low concentrations of radioactive materials with long half-lives. Tailings contain radium (which, through radioactive decay, becomes radon), thorium, and small residual amounts of uranium that were not extracted during the milling process.

The Rio Algom uranium mill and tailings site in Utah is undergoing reclamation.

LOCATIONS OF URANIUM MILL TAILINGS SITES

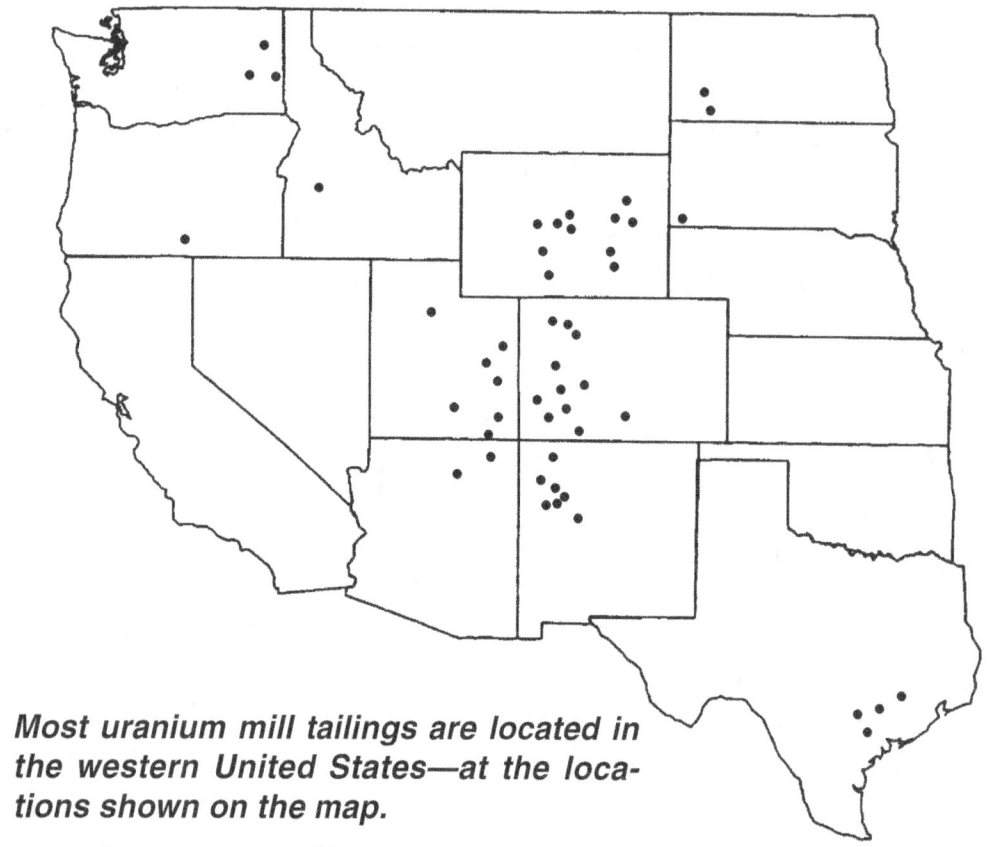

Most uranium mill tailings are located in the western United States—at the locations shown on the map.

The Office of Surface Mining, U.S. Department of Interior and individual states regulate mining. NRC regulates milling and the disposal of tailings in non-Agreement States, while State agencies regulate these activities in Agreement States when the agreement specifically includes tailings.

Mill tailings consist of fine-grained, sand-like and silty materials, usually deposited in large piles next to the mill that processed the ore. Uranium mills are located principally in the western United States, where deposits of uranium ore are more plentiful.

NRC requires licensees to meet Environmental Protection Agency standards for cleanup of uranium and thorium mill sites after the milling operations have permanently closed. This includes requirements for long-term stability of the mill tailings piles, radon emissions control, water quality protection and cleanup, and cleanup of lands and buildings.

NRC regulations require that a cover be placed over the mill tailings to control the release of radon gases at the end of milling operations. The cover must be effective in controlling radon releases for 1,000 years to the extent reasonably achievable and, in any case, for no less than 200 years.

The uranium mill tailings contain chemical and radiological material discarded from the mill. Radium and thorium, which are the dominant radioactive materials in mill tailings, have long half-lives (1,600 and 77,000 years respectively). Therefore Congress requires perpetual government custody of the tailings disposal sites.

For Additional Information Contact:

Office of Public Affairs—Headquarters
U.S. Nuclear Regulatory Commission
Washington, DC 20555

Telephone: 301-415-8200
Fax: 301-415-2234
Internet: opa@nrc.gov
website: www.nrc.gov

Regional Public Affairs Offices

Region I   475 Allendale Road
                      King of Prussia, PA 19406-1415
                      (610) 337-5330

Region II   61 Forsyth Street
                      Suite 23 T85
                      Atlanta, GA 30303-3415
                      (404) 562-4416

Region III   801 Warrenville Road
                      Lisle, IL 60532-4351
                      (630) 829-9663

Region IV   611 Ryan Plaza Drive
                      Suite 400
                      Arlington, TX 76011-8064
                      (817) 860-8128

U.S. Nuclear Regulatory Commission

Washington, DC 20555-0001

Office of Public Affairs

NUREG/BR-0216, Rev. 2
May 2002